Journal

MW01602167

Copyright © 2

Published by Leslie Lynn Reilly

Printed in the United States of America

Contact Info: maukagirl@hushmail.com

ISBN: 9798495517844

Other Books by Leslie Reilly:

When Cancer Calls, Love Answers
A Girl Who Loves Naia
Deanie Dolphin Coloring Book for Kids
Santa's Christmas Coloring Book for Kids
Follow Your Dreams - Journal
Activity Book for Seniors
Follow Your Heart, Live Your Dreams Notebook

You, yourself, as much as anyone in the entire universe, deserve your

Love & Affection

~ Buddha

───────────────────

───────────────────

Eagle's Eye

Design Your Life With Clarity and Purpose

Made in the USA
Columbia, SC
29 October 2021